# Persistence

*poems by*

# Ruth McArthur

*Finishing Line Press*
Georgetown, Kentucky

# Persistence

*To Mama, Grandma Katie
and the others
This work would never have come to be without the careful reading, hard questions, thoughtful suggestions and general literary midwifery of my writing group—
Julie Martin, Robin Greenler, Jan Stanton
and of course Sarah Sadie.
Many thanks.*

Copyright © 2020 by Ruth McArthur
ISBN 978-1-64662-139-2 First Edition
All rights reserved under International and Pan-American Copyright Conventions. No part of this book may be reproduced in any manner whatsoever without written permission from the publisher, except in the case of brief quotations embodied in critical articles and reviews.

## ACKNOWLEDGMENTS

"Sassy" was published in altered form in *Voices de la Luna* under the name Ruth Francis.

Publisher: Leah Maines
Editor: Christen Kincaid
Cover Art: Cecilia Fuentes
Author Photo: Randy Fuentes
Cover Design: Elizabeth Maines McCleavy

Printed in the USA on acid-free paper.
Order online: www.finishinglinepress.com
also available on amazon.com

      Author inquiries and mail orders:
            Finishing Line Press
              P. O. Box 1626
       Georgetown, Kentucky 40324
                U. S. A.

# Table of Contents

Persistence ........................................................................... 1

*Section 1: Ida*
News Source ........................................................................ 2
Stitched Together ................................................................ 3
Sweet Life ............................................................................ 4
Sassy .................................................................................... 5
Helping Hand ..................................................................... 6
Washing Machines ............................................................. 7
On Having a Laundress for a Wife .................................. 8
Relief .................................................................................... 9
Escape ................................................................................ 10
Return ................................................................................ 12
Waste .................................................................................. 13
Willene and Hugh ............................................................. 14

*Section 2: A Place Untouched by Language*
Subterranean .................................................................... 16
Descending ....................................................................... 17
The Abyss .......................................................................... 19
Calling It Out ................................................................... 20
Duty Done ........................................................................ 21

*Section 3: The Others*
The Two, Tangoing .......................................................... 22
Firebirds ............................................................................ 23
Wild Waltz ........................................................................ 24
Diminuendo ..................................................................... 25
Lament .............................................................................. 26
Fatherly Love .................................................................... 27
Dead Woman in the Company Cabin ........................... 28
Cinderella ......................................................................... 29
Prospects ........................................................................... 30
Bonanza ............................................................................ 31

*Section 4: Warp and Weft*
Breakage ............................................................................ 32
Can the Paradigm Shift? ................................................. 33
Tightrope .......................................................................... 34
For the Women ................................................................ 35

*Appendix: Family Tree ........................................................ 36*

## Persistence

### I.

The silhouette of the barn swallow
against the evening sky
is odd.

Adhered crosswise to its tail is
the feather of a much larger bird,
at least as long as the swallow.

The swallow perches on the power wire,
pecks, preens itself persistently,
almost frantically.

### II.

Surely the bird will be dead under the wire this morning.
How can it fly dragging such extra weight?
Or catch insects on the wing
or escape the red-shouldered hawk
who regularly patrols the area?

But there is no corpse.
A shadow crosses the ground—
the blighted bird,
flying,
a bit wobbly,
but flying.
All morning it swoops
with the other swallows.

### III.

By evening, the swallow has re-mastered
the art,
flitting about with no detectable lack of grace,
swooping
from the nest above the front door
to hunt,
returning to feed the young,
huge burden still attached.

It has learned to carry on.

# Section I:
# Ida

---

**News Source**
  *1973*

She loved her soap operas, did Ida. Stories,
she called them: *The Edge of Night, Secret Storm.*
My grandmother parked herself on the sofa with
her crochet work in hand before the creepy chords

of these over-wrought shows began. A young girl's kidnapping
worried her no end—the searchers would come so close
and then a strange concatenation of circumstances
would misdirect them! The poor girl's parents had to be

beside themselves! Another character died tragically (of course).
Ida's tears were as sincere as though it had been a family member.
Thus, her tears were bitter and heartfelt when in May 1973,
networks across the country began gavel to gavel coverage of

the Watergate hearings. *They won't keep it up! Who would watch such as that?*
Keep it up they did, to her fury. *They just up an' quit showin' my stories.*

But there was her crochet, and she had to watch something,
so watch she did. Just a little bit. And she wouldn't like it—it wouldn't last forever.
And then. She skipped depression and leapt straight into acceptance.
Delighted, wholehearted, committed acceptance. Could hardly

take a break for lunch. Why, this was much better than her stories!
This was money and power and cheating and lying at a level to which
her stories could not dream of achieving! Dastardly government men
getting their comeuppance. She preferred Howard Baker's way

of conducting business (*such kind eyes*) to that of Sam Ervin
(*them eyebrows look like caterpillars playin' on his face*).
Dinnertime conversation switched from a litany of woes
of preposterous fictional characters to exhaustive accounts
of who did what, who knew what, when they knew it. *Bad, bad men,
ever one of 'em.* This woman's education had ended at age twelve.
Never picked up a book since other than to dust under it,
yet she kept my professor father better informed than the local newspaper.

**Stitched Together**
*Ida, 1920*

The saddest brown eyes you ever saw
gaze out of the photo.

A woman in a lace-edged dress, her wedding dress.
But there will be no wedding, him already married.

She made the trappings of one—
a dress, a photo to send for folks back home.

This woman can make do, turn nothing
into a bit of something. She is a quilter.

A darner of socks. A patcher of pants. She will piece
and mend this as well. Make a tattered "marriage"

with this man. Because she is pregnant.
There must be a "wedding" to make it seem right.

But it isn't right. She won't shame her Jesus,
won't enter His holy house ever again.

Brown eyes, saddest you ever saw.

**Sweet Life**
    *Ida, 1924*

He had some money from selling his land out west.
We moved closer home,
set up an ice cream shop.
Bought it whole entire—the shop,
them little round tables, curly iron chairs.

I scrubbed the building,
made red-checked cushions for them dainty chairs.
Beau and Willene toddled and crawled
on the black and white tile floor I worked so hard on.
Played with other children what come in.

We done right well.
But then George got the sugar diabetes,
needs shots and that costs money,
which we got no extra of right now.
He can't work so hard no more.
I got them two younguns.
He done the books and numbers,
say we best sell.

So he done took the money,
bought a patch of land.
We can have a goat and chickens
and a vegetable patch. We can eat.
He'll think of something to do for cash money.
He say.
We gonna be all right.
So he say.

**Sassy**
   *Willene, 1930*

My mama talked to the teacher, told her
I'd be wearin' Beau's old overalls 'cause she don't
have money for cloth to make a dress like the rules say.
Teacher says that's fine, for me to wear overalls til things look up.

The girls at recess teased me 'cause the overalls
are patched on the behind.
I knew I was gonna cry so I turned my back on them.
Then they laughed at how many patches there is,
'cause one of the patches is patched
so I wagged my behind at them an' sung out,
*My mama makes better patches than your mama*
til teacher called us in.

She moved me from second grade bench to third grade bench
on account of I done read what they done read
an' pitch in when they do they spelling an' ciphers
an' never miss a one.

**Helping Hand**
*1930*

Down at the grocery, Ida tries to buy flour and lard.
*You owe too much already, haven't paid a penny on it.*
*You aren't the only ones on hard times.* The grocer's voice is loud.
Ida grabs Willene's hand to leave.

*Mama, how we gonna make biscuits with no flour nor lard?*
Ida's other hand involuntarily touches her bruised cheek, drops.
*C'mon, sugar.* On the porch, Judge Riley's wife catches up
to them. *His hand that did that, Ida?* Gesturing

to the other woman's bruise. No answer from Ida,
but Willene chirps *Yes'm.* Ida throws a sour look at her daughter.
Mrs. Riley takes her arm, guides her down the stairs.
*My Johnetta cut her arm bad chopping wood.*

*Can't do my washing any more. Can I send Skeet around with*
 *my old washing machine? Best the Sears Catalog had when I married.*
*You do my washing, I would be happy to give you 50 cents a week for it.*
*Can you help me?*

Ida shuffles, mumbles, *I reckon.* Mrs. Riley gives
Ida fifty cents on account. Ida waits til the judge's wife and
her man Skeet leave before hurrying inside the store.
In the dust, Willene does a quiet dance on her skinny legs.

**Washing Machines**
*1930*

After twenty years' hard use, the paint is chipped and worn
but the name *Quick and Easy* still shows.
It is the finest appliance Ida has ever seen.
A big tub at one end—
fill it with a bit of soap,
hot water from the fire,
add the clothes,
stir with a paddle.
Move the clothes to the spiral wringer,
wring them out.
Bring more water from the fire,
refill the tub with rinsing water.

Run the clothes through the wringer again.
Hang them up on the line.
Willene has dragged bucket after bucket of hot water.
Unless it rains, they're ready to iron by afternoon.

After the midday meal of beans, biscuits and gravy,
Ida sets to heating the iron at the fire.
She explains to Willene how to get the iron hot enough
to do the job but not so hot as to leave a scorch.
Ida finds tears in some of Judge Riley's handkerchiefs,
sets Willene to mending.
Teaches her how to darn up holes in the socks,
patch the knees in the little boy's trousers.
Nine years old and the girl is a wizard with needle and thread.

Before the week is out, Doc Andrews' wife
and Pastor Sheffield's wife have sent their washing
along with stories of their missing or injured servant girls.
Would Ida be good enough to help them out?

Ida doesn't study these stories too hard,
just builds her fire every morning,
totes water,
washes clothes,
feeds her children.

## On Having a Laundress for a Wife
*1930*

George sees the fire in the yard,
the cauldron of water,
the wringer washer,
the porch filled with other people's
shirts,
undergarments,
bedlinens.

Grabbing his wife by the arm,
he brings her face to his.
This time,
she does not cower.

*They's hungry.* She nods
at the children playing
in the dust.

He flings her back.
She narrowly misses the fire.

*You are never to speak to me again.*
*Be sure my supper isn't cold.*

**Relief**
        *Ida, 1936*

Times so bad people ain't
sendin' they washin' out no more,
not to no one.

But I still got mouths to feed.
Can't find no kinda work
an' George, he don't try,
just sits an' jaws on the porch.

So I walked to the county seat
an' got the Relief money
the president is givin' to folk.
George, he cain't countenance it,

say no one in his family gonna beg
nor take charity. Well, I ain't
gonna pretend as I am his family,
not no more. Ole Doc Andrews

is in need of a housekeeper,
he say I can come and bring
Chip with me. Willene listened
to George's sweet lies and is staying.
Ain't never gettin' Beau away.

**Escape**
*Willene, 1937*

Darkening clouds, lowering, heavy, seal in
the heat, push it down. It smothers her.
The chickens mill about. The last few
runner beans are yellowing. Time to plant
for a fall crop to be ready before
the first November cold snap.
But she's not studying to plant more,
let alone harvest, put up a fall batch
to see them through the winter,
nor care for those chickens.
She is done with all that.

George's sweet-talking ways, his bombast—
she likes that word, bombast—
have no more magic. He is a liar. He will never
let her set up shop sewing to earn her own money.
Nor never so much as lift a finger
to work like he'd promised nor make Beau
chop wood. But most of all, he is never
going to quit what he'd promised to quit.
That sorry business—and now Beau has started in.

No, she is done with them. Those fifty miles
over to Mama seem as far as the moon. But if she dies
on the way, she dies. Might as well be dead if she stays.

Leaves on the pecan tree over by the outhouse flutter,
then blow in the freshening wind. Pines across the road shimmy,
limber as Mama's zinnias. Now they toss their tops,

holy rollers at a tent revival. Fat drops fall,
marking the dusty yard with deep, rimmed depressions.
George and Beau, down at the foundry trading
scrap iron for nickels, will no more walk home
in this downpour than that 'ere chicken might
recite The 23rd Psalm.

Cornbread, a jar of beans fall into her apron pocket.
Pouring rain now. She'll be soaked to the skin in no time.
George's oilskin coat hangs on the door hook

but he'll beat her if she borrows it. Realizing
he isn't going to have a chance to beat her,
she nearly cracks a grin.
Nearly.

More cornbread, jars of beans go in the coat pockets
And a fork. Pulls the coat over her head. Steps off
the porch into the deluge, across to the piney woods.
She will be well shed of the place with no scent for the dog
before they ever know she is gone.

**Return**
    *Ida, 1937*

I what but dropped the flour bin
when Chip come runnin' in to say
*Willene's comin' through the back yard*

but sure enough, yonder she was
in George's oiled coat, skinny, dirty,
lookin' as though she been wrung out.

Hugged my neck as she never has done,
says can I stay here and go to school
and help with chores.
Doc is a good enough man to say sure.

**Waste Paper**
*Willene, 1937*

Mama and me both told Doc Andrews
not to bother letting George know where I am.
Waste of his good paper and ink.
But he must have anyway because
gathering trash to burn, I find a note
from George in Doc's wastebasket.
Doesn't care what happens to me,
never wants to hear about me
ever again. Only surprise is
he paid actual cash money
for a postage stamp.

There's drizzle.
On the way to the burn barrel
I put on his oilskin coat
that I took when I left.
Pitch the trash into the flaming barrel,
then the coat.

The flames stutter, then they catch.
Evil smelling black smoke rises,
wafts up to the overcast sky,
showing black against the grey.
Higher yet the smoke rises,
to where the clouds seem to be thinning
at last.

**Willene and Hugh**
  *1987*

As he rises from bed, the feet startle him:
purple, thick-veined, toenails
yellow and thick. But attached to him.
Combing his hair, an old man looks
out from the mirror, as puzzled as he.
*Remember to shave*, she calls down the hall.

Slowed by an arthritic leg, Willene cooks two eggs,
four strips of turkey bacon. Glances at the clock
shaped like a frying pan.

Coffee goes into yellow mugs bought
with Green Stamps fifty years before,
juice into tiny glasses, courtesy of
a gas station frequent buyer program.

She lays breakfast before him,
their ancient sacrament.
He folds the newspaper, thanks her
and God for their daily bread,
their many blessings.

Pictures of children smile down at the table.
She has him recite the name of each
daughter and son, no longer asking him to name
the grandchildren.

She has him tell stories:
of his grandparents' Kansas farm,
his teenaged escapade with the merliton tree,
a dance in college, the last before Pearl Harbor,
his buddy the navigator from the flight crew
who drew insolent cartoons.
His eyes clear as he speaks.
These memories are near—
their love was fresh, bodies unblemished.

He finishes his toast,
the cloud falls.
He wipes his mouth with

the paper napkin.

*Love you,* he says, shuffling
as he carries his empty plate to the kitchen.
*Be sure to rinse the egg off before
you put that plate in the dishwasher*, she calls.

# Section 2:
# A Place Untouched by Language

---

**Subterranean**

When I removed encroaching Ashe juniper,
a sandy wasteland remained.
I prayed for a miracle. Seasons came, went.
Still I prayed.
Sotol sprang up, shoots reaching for the sky.
Grasses appeared from nowhere.

Bearing ancient information,
dormant seeds
from a hidden seed bank
came to life.

At four months gestation,
a female fetus has developed
all the eggs she will ever have.
Thus, I was inside my mother
Willene who was inside Ida,
absorbing
physical genetic material
along with Ida's environment,
physical and emotional.

I had known George after all—
deep in my being
in a place untouched
by language.

## Descending
### 1887, Vermont, Rose, age 12

Lord knows, I am doing my level best
to keep things together here.
Mother can't.
Just sits by the fire mooning and wailing
since Flora died, that baby puking up her
own shit again and again, clutching her belly
and sobbing between pukes. Mother leaving it
to me to clean that mess whilst she held Flora
and put poultices on the baby's stomach.
For days
and days and days
til she goes still
and dies.

Doc comes and pronounces her dead,
says to Poppa, *you ought to have called for me earlier,*
but we all know he couldn't have done anything,
never can. Just charges us money.
Couldn't do anything
for little Fanny either once she got
the sugar diabetes,
she just lay there weak and cried
for more water
but too much wasn't
even enough.

And Poppa couldn't be bothered
either time
but just drank when he came
home from the shoe peg factory,
pestering Mother, saying
there was enough noise
at the factory he didn't need all this
mewling and whimpering but just wanted
one flat minute to hear his own thoughts.
Well after both those burials it sure is quiet.
George and Jessie run free in the woods.
Mother just stares.

Then one morning Poppa walked in the coop
where I was gathering eggs and told me to bend
over the feed rack and did business with me
and said if I didn't like it
I could pray to God til he was done.
But there is no God.

**The Abyss**

*Ellen, Vermont, 1889*
First my two youngest died.
Flora with a griping in her bowel,
then not six months later,
Fanny from sugar diabetes.
Both miserable deaths.
The first could keep nothing in,
the other couldn't get enough water
if we drowned her.
Wailing and crying to tear your heart out,
no way to help. My heart is so heavy
I am nailed to my chair, cannot get up
to save my soul. Thank God for Rose,
such a helper, taking my place in every way.

*Ellen, 1892*
My grief has finally lifted only
to have sorrow
rush in once again like a flood.
My son Jessie has the sugar diabetes.
His brother George cannot bear it.
Those two share a soul.
Never see one that you don't see the other.
George is the brains. And the mischief.
Jessie's sweet kindness keeps a balance.
When George isn't by his brother's bed
bringing water, begging and bargaining
for him to live, he is wild in the forest,
grieving his heart out, coming back so vile
and wretched he's hardly human.
When Jessie dies, both my sons will be gone.

*Ellen, 1898*
Sure enough, I've not seen my George
since his brother's death. In his grief,
he and Rose had a fight about something,
I don't know what. Al T said
he is no longer welcome here. George
kissed me, and left. My heart breaks
yet again. He is a shell of himself,
a man with a shattered heart.
He needs a wife.

**Calling It Out**
    *Rose, 1900*

Needs a wife, my hind foot! A tramp, more like.
Mother can't see through his complaining
when he writes home. How no one
appreciates his intellect.
The bosses never like him.
Not at the marble quarry,
not at the shoe peg factory,
not at the sawmill.

Years on end, that good-for-nothing
brother of mine has crisscrossed
the State of Vermont looking for work.
Mother wails that he never visits,
forgetting the row he and Poppa had.
To her, he is just a poor, misunderstood boy.
Man of twenty-six, he is!
Mother thinks the Navy will appreciate
his intelligence. Me, I think he is wanted
for a crime, or gotten a girl in a family way,
for him to risk years of constant toil on
a Navy ship.

## Duty Done
### *Rose, 1941*

Mother has passed at last.
Most of her days on this earth spent grieving,
weighted down by the deaths of her young children.
Too much for a person to bear, and she couldn't.

And not a day has gone by
since before the turn of the century
that she didn't mourn the loss of her precious George.
Not that he died, more's the pity,
but he left forty years ago, never returned.
Oh how she has made me feel her bereavement,
as if it is my fault what he did
that made Poppa run him off.

Didn't she wail with loneliness in the long stretches
with no word from him?
And didn't she rejoice the few letters he wrote?
When she received that huge photo from the Navy,
the crew on the ship, George on the rigging,
you'd have thought Christ had come again.
She propped that thing on the mantel,
prattled on about it til Poppa said
put it away or he would burn it.

I never saw it again. Til today,
when I searched her wardrobe
for her fine dress for burial.
There at the bottom, under that dress
lay that wretched photo.
I guess it has mouldered there these forty years.
But George's face has been cut out.
Ages ago—the edges of the tear are soft,
delicate as butterfly wings.

Then what do I find in her dresser drawer
but that silver locket she never let anyone see.
Whose picture do you suppose is there
but her precious George.
Cut from the Navy photo,
scowling his meanness out at the world.

Mother, I have done for you all could.
I am burying you both.

# Section 3: The Others

### The Two, Tangoing
*Gladys, 1907*

Good looking fellow sat at my lunch counter,
just off the train.
Looking for a place to stay.
I tell him I am up from Fox Hollow
just three weeks ago.
He grins big at that.
I tell him I am staying at Mrs. Sykes'.
How I love Gatesville,
all the folks to meet here at the café.
How I am learning quality manners
like how to set a table and fold napkins.
Stanley, for that is his name,
tells me he can tell I am quality,
is surprised I need teaching
though I am just sixteen.

Stanley finds me at the boarding house
every evening after my shift.
We sit on Mrs. Sykes' porch and rock.
I tell him about how Pa drinks,
can't hardly make a go with the farm.
Stanley *tsks*, says that is foolish,
that he has better things to do
with his money than swallow it down
out of a bottle.

He tells me about cold winters in Vermont,
how he joined the Navy, has sailed the seven seas.
And oh does he have tales of all the strange lands
and naked savages. Mrs. Sykes takes peeks at us
through the curtain but we just laugh and have a good time.

**Firebirds**
    *Gladys*

After a week or so,
Stanley is tired of Mrs. Sykes' snooping,
says it isn't funny anymore, we are not children.
He collects his hat from the newel post on the porch steps
and we go walking.
Past the café,
past the Methodist church
past the town square,
past the Presbyterian church.
First holding hands,
then him wrapping his arms around me.
Even planted a kiss, which I did not mind at all
and gave back to him hearty.
Oh, his eyes lit up with that.
Said his boarding house
was just around the corner,
did I want to go upstairs,
see his treasures from Navy days.
Well, I did and one thing led to another and
unless you are dull as dust
you know what that was.

**Wild Waltz**
        *Gladys, 1907*

Walking down Main Street to work,
who should jump me but Ma,
here to take me home.
Being a sight stronger than her,
I busted away easy
but who should be right there but Pa,
liquored up as usual for this time of day.

They marched me to the train station
intending to take me back to Fox Hollow,
but ole Pa can't think straight on a good day
and left me on a bench
while he went to get the tickets.
Of course I took off.

Stanley and I gathered our few things but quick,
hid in the Methodist church
where no one will ever think to look,
and took a train for Boston next morning.
On the way to get married by the justice of the peace,
he told me his name is George, not Stanley.
I told him I am in the family way.

**Diminuendo**
    *Gladys, 1909*

We came home to Ma and Pa
since they want me back so bad.
But George has little time for farm chores
what with being a big man on the post office porch,
having a fine old time with all who can spare a moment.
Which seems to be only men. I am just commenting.

Meanwhile, I am scrambling to keep the garden going
and some chickens to provide for little Jessie
and the baby due next month.
George calls me dirty and ugly,
that I have a sassy mouth,
when what I am is run ragged
and baby-swollen.

**Lament**
        *Gladys, 1910*

George was as uninterested in baby Irene
as he was over the moon about little Jessie.
Not that that ever got him to bring in food or money.
Which I pointed out more than once.
He pushed me into the wall,
called me a harpy and
he would not put up with such.
Grabbed Jessie and took off.

The old biddies in town say
he took that Fletcher "widow" with him,
her and her two young'uns.
I say good luck and good riddance.
But it has been a year.

I would like to have my son back.

**Fatherly Love**
    *Bertha Fletcher, 1910*

i.
We'll stake a claim out west, George says. Live free,
beholden to none. No more washing pots,
taking slaps on my rear and more at the boarding house.
And he does make me laugh with his fine talk.

Left yesterday with him and his Jessie,
taken from that nagging harridan while
she hoed the garden with the new infant
by her. I didn't want to take Jessie,

he not two years old but George says a man
can't leave his first-born son. Must raise his boy
himself, teach him the ways of the world.
I love him for his solid character, how he sticks

to what a father ought to be. He'll be father
to my two little ones too.

ii.
Riding the rails, sleeping among the crates,
the floor cold and hard against us, clatter
of the wheels so loud and steady as to

drive all thought from our minds. Little Jessie
crying. We jump out every so often
to glean food from farmers, so he calls it.

Stealing, I say. I've done things in my life
I shouldn't but never took what wasn't mine.
He laughs at my scruples, whatever they are,

and reminds me we are doing it
for his precious Jessie. Where is all that
money he says he had from
working at the railroad?

iii.
Hopped off in Little Rock as that Jessie
was fading to nothing. He cried for
his mother and water to the last breath.
George sat by the boarding house bed a long time,
for once with no words. Nor tears, but a grieved
face as I hope never again to see.

## Dead Woman in the Company Cabin
*Colorado, 1914*

Your name is lost. We don't know
your age. Did you live near the mines?
Or did he bring you there? Did he even

pretend to marry you? Did it matter?
Were you a young girl, fresh hopes
in your heart? Or were you seasoned,

realistic? Knew you needed a man to
share the hard, bitter life in the San Juans?
Were you in love? Was he? Did you

have children together? Where are they?
Did he beat you like the others? Did you fall,
strike your head? Or did you die of cold?

Illness? Was there a quarrel?
Was there always a quarrel?
How long did you lie in the cabin,

dead and alone, before you were found?
Was there anyone to mourn you?

I mourn you now.

**Cinderella**
      *Mavis, San Juan Mountains, Colorado 1914*

Aunt Sue can't be right about the woman in the cabin
is dead by Mr. George Meachum's hand. He is far too kind.
The way he bows over my hand in greeting,
carries the mop pail when he sees me slaving

here at the bar—not that he is a drinker, just
nowhere else to go. Says my aunt works me
like Cinderella and like Cinderella
I am not made for such—too pretty and fine.

Aunt Sue certainly would not agree. Only reason
she took me in is I was big enough to work
and she works me hard. Watches me close,
keeps me from any fun I might have. Scowls

when Mr. Meachum laughs with me,
sniffs at his fine words.
Must be she wants him for herself but
who wants a tough old bird like her?

He is a wise man, fought in the Navy,
sailed around the world and is a war hero.
And educated, calls the evening light
*crepuscular* and such.

So when he came for me in a hurry to leave here
and mine for gold in the Arizona mountains
of course I did. I will be sixteen in the fall
and know my own mind.

**Prospects**
       *Mavis, Arizona, 1914*

We got off the train in Globe, Arizona.
Spent a few days talking with folks,
filed a claim on land north of here.
Sheep and cattle country but best of all
prospecting. George says we will hunt for gold,
live like royalty.

He being a decent man
and it being Sunday,
he found us a justice of the peace
and we married before we left out of here.
Someone made our picture,
which made him mad.
We took off for the hills on our mule.

**Bonanza**
> *Mavis, Arizona 1916*

No gold yet. Just a tent
with a bed,
cookpot
and fire pit.
One baby,
another on the way.

George up at the sawmill
five days and nights a week.
Feels that is enough of a contribution,
to our life. That and the babies.

He's not a man to tote water, fetch wood.
Sometimes catches a fish in the stream.
If it suits him.
But not if it doesn't.

Yet he complains about the smell
of the tent, that which was old when we got it,
and how I haven't looked for gold in earnest
and made our fortunes for him.

When I had something to say about that
he shoved me. I landed close to the fire,
he went to kicking my belly.
Didn't lose the baby
but won't it be a surprise for him
when he gets back next week
to find we are gone.

Big as I am, I am walking
out of here, me and little Edna.

# Section Four: Warp and Weft

---

**Breakage**
    *2018*

The pump on the water well is broken.
The internet is down.
The headlines of the day are galling.
A recent quarrel with a friend jangles
like glass fragments.

Darrell the well man remembers my two large dogs,
is sorry to hear they are gone. Quick adjustments
and the water flows.

The internet man beams, his grin impossibly wide,
sweetly goofy. Asks after my daughter.
That she now has two children makes him feel old, he says.
In a bit of serendipity, his name is Jesus.

My friend and I set a coffee date to talk things out.

These. These are the mundane tasks of
knitting broken bits toward wholeness.

**Can the Paradigm Shift?**

Masses of robins overhead in the prairie
stun me to stillness. They boil
out of the forest, swarm over the creek,
fly above the little grassland.

Head back, eyes on the sky, I segment
the first wave into fives, tens, fifties,
then finally hundreds. Maybe thousands.
More. More. More.

How many centuries have they massed here,
fed, flown on? Knowledge implanted in their very DNA.
Behavior repeated over and over and over and over.

What if the behavior ceases to serve them?

Might the creative act of a single bird
save the entire rabble of robins?

**Tightrope**
*1951*

My father believed that no one, no matter how horrible,
was beyond redemption. They had the two little girls now,
they must make an effort to reconcile with George.

Willene was tenuous and raw on the topic.
The ugly history with her father could never be excused.
Some wounds don't heal.

And those precious little girls, trotting
ahead of the adults, unaware of any tensions.
George being near them turned her stomach.

Now they were having Sunday dinner with her in-laws.
Even without her father's predatory history,
Willene was jumpy with worry about the event.

Because George had the unfortunate habit
of ridiculing women he deemed ugly.
To their faces. Loudly. Laughingly.

With high-falutin' verbiage. The more hurt a woman was,
the more he reviled her. Her mother-in-law was tall,
skinny, ungainly with an odd, lurching walk. And frankly,

not pretty at all—huge nose, planes and angles
of her long face somehow off kilter.
Which you immediately forgot because her piercing,

twinkling blue eyes, large warm smile were all for you.
She suffered no nonsense, was unflinchingly kind.
Willene couldn't bear the thought of her being hurt.

Who knows what transpired at that visit?
But on the walk home, George turned
a gentled and humbled face to Willene.

*That is a beautiful woman.*

**For The Women**

For the starry eyed young women,
flattered by the attentions of a man;

For the women, young but careworn,
with dreams of escape;

For the women tired of drudgery,
of menial work who want someone,
anyone, to smile at them,
laugh with them, touch their hair,
desperately wanting their own home, their own children;

For the women who take slaps
and insults because there is nowhere to turn;

For the women whose love sours,
who find it never was love;

For the women who are lied to;

For the women who find a way
to feed and clothe their children no matter what;

For the women who leave and never come back;

For the abandoned women who call themselves widows
hoping they can marry again;

For the women who dream of something more,
not knowing what;

For the women who dream of peace;

For the women who mend trousers, cuffs, hems,
broken dishes, broken windows, their lives.

For all the women.

## Appendix: FAMILY TREE

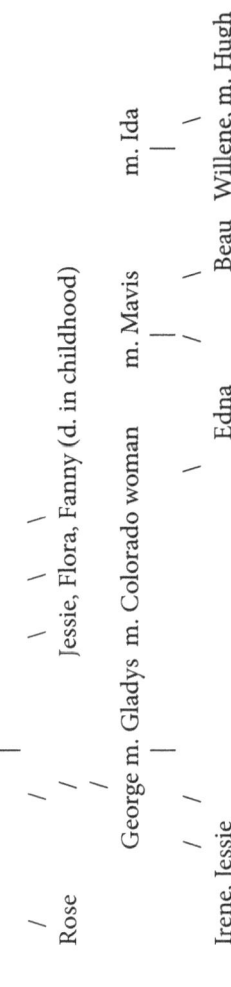

www.ingramcontent.com/pod-product-compliance
Lightning Source LLC
LaVergne TN
LVHW041556070426
835507LV00011B/1123